Mighty Good Land

MIGHTY GOOD LAND

POEMS BY
DAN POWERS

black greyhound media
Nashville, Tennessee

Some of these poems first appeared in the following publications:

Number One
Old Hickory Review
Cumberland Poetry Review
New York Quarterly
Roanoke Review
Riverrun
Zone 3
ART/LIFE
Alura
Poem
River City
Sure
Apalachee Quarterly
Plains Poetry Journal
What To Say When We're Not Speaking (chapbook)
Witness (chapbook)
Abraxas
The Penny Dreadful Review

"Lilith" is based on a poem of the same name by Ron Koertge.

Book design by MER Images. Cover illustration by Mary Reaves Uhles.

First Edition
10   9   8   7   6   5   4   3   2   1

ISBN-13: 978-0-9706371-1-6
ISBN-10: 0-9706371-1-X

Black Greyhound Media
P.O. Box 40367
Nashville, Tennessee 37204

www.blackgreyhoundmedia.com

This book of poems is dedicated to all my family, especially my wife, Cheryl, who fails to see anything but good in me. And to my father, who tried to show me the way.

Contents

Aching Hands

God, If You Are There

Enough

Acknowledgments

About the Author

Index of First Lines

What hath a man of all his labor, and of the vexation of his heart wherein he hath labored under the sun?

– Ecclesiastes

Chapter 1

Good Earth and Poor

Morels

Two years ago, my friend Vantrease
said farming would not pay his bills.
He sold his milk cows and leased
the Sears catalog store in town.

Blackberry vines and sumac
crowd his unkept pasture and the fences sag.
Last week at church, he held out his hands
soft and white for us to see and said,
"A farm is like the strength in a man's hands.
You try hard to keep it, and you lose it."

In the trillium beneath the hickory grove
on our ridge, my son and I find a few morels
and drop them into a brown paper bag.
Our small talk worn thin, we walk back toward the house
through the dew-wet pasture without speaking.

Here, miles from town, without his friends to see,
he reaches across our silent striding
and grasps my hand with all the strength
of his ten years.

Each of us holds on.

The Sun Reminds Me of Being in a Chevy

Riding the dips on Lakeshore Drive,
we fractured the air at 60 miles an hour
in my brother's Chevrolet, souped up
on a fifth of screwdriver and knowing
beneath the front seat was a gross of condoms—
a box of willing miracles,
each one soft and simmering in its own gold foil.

We were dancing seventeen and ready.
We were tuned for excitement, for fast cars
with four-barrel carbs and four speeds in the floor,
for dips and curves and women.
Always we rode that last long turn
after firing through the slot
with rubber squealing, teeth clenched,
us all leaning hard
to the inside of the curve.
It was almost more than those retread tires
from Jack's Garage could take.

On Sundays we would ride to church dressed up,
walk in with the sweet smell of motor oil
and car wax in the air around us,
the incense of our true sanctuary:
the smoky church of polished chrome,
glowing dials, tinted glass, rock and roll
and rolled and pleated leather.
The wing of the church had theater seats
where we would sing the hymns,
pretend to hear the sermon, and I'd take off one shoe
and slide my foot into the seat in front

and find Paula Goodnight's ass with my toes.
I'd think about those rubbers waiting outside in the car
and I knew God would strike me dead
or my brother in Vietnam, or my dog.

Paula got pregnant by Bobby Green,
had an abortion down in Birmingham
and came back with religion
just before we wrecked that car
one slick night in a vodka curve above the river.
When my father came to pull us from the ditch,
he never said a word
about those shining packages of gold
falling from the car with flakes of tinted glass.

We pooled the money we had left
and bought an ancient English Ford,
rebuilt it in Jack's Garage.
Even with Jack's help, it would not do 50
in a strong tail wind.
And though we often talked about it,
that old green Chevy never ran again.
After twenty years it still waits
behind my father's barn—
chrome flecked with rust,
leather seats filled with chicken shit,
the whole thing wrapped in kudzu.

The headlights stare across the pasture,
the grill hangs in toothless grin,
wind still whistles through the side vents

and cobwebs fly like Paula's hair.
The metal ticks in summer's rising heat,
and among the bits of broken glass
the sun gleams bright and hard,
sometimes gold, fracturing the air.

Good Earth and Poor

For years my father ran from the Depression
and almost made a living
pulling wrenches against the stubborn stems of valves,
finger calipers and standard/metric rule
in oil-stained khaki.
In the evenings around our table,
the kitchen-steamed walls and windows sweating,
he would dream his dream aloud
and speak the promise to himself and us
about a hundred-acre piece of land
he knew in Neely's Bend.
Then he would laugh and turn his pockets inside out
to teach us empty.
If he only had the money—land was cheap then.

One spring he built a small wood boat
and took us fishing in the bend of the river,
taught us how to hold the hook in our minds,
and floating in the current,
we watched the shoreline pass
and learned discernment, good earth from poor.

He paid my way to ag school and settled
for two and a half acres in the middle of the bend,
a stand of walnuts on the hill
and earth black in the center
for a garden that would grow tomatoes,
beans, and sweet corn—where his motion,
wheeled in the order of those green rows,
was more of grace and dance than toil,
and the song that carried him

lifted us from any burden he bore
across the green curve of his little world
that in years became enough:

The seasons and the planting of the seed—
by nature the true work of our father—
who never owned the piece of land he wanted,
but it was near, past the end of our field,
and through the seasons he watched it fall
piece by piece into the hands of subdividers.
And with the half-smile of given-up desire,
he would say, "That was mighty good land."
And he would say it softly to no one but himself
while he held his hands dug deep into his pockets.

Drought

The blue haze and long shadows of the morning
bake into the hum and click of bright July.
The forecast is the same as yesterday's, last week's:
another day to fry and blur the air
crackling the lespedeza in our pasture.

Four years without rain. It's hard to watch
our pond shrivel to its center, an open wound
in our farm dying in the heat.

A station wagon full of friends
from the farm up the road
wobbles past us in the sun,
like our knobby cattle wobbling to the shade.
Road maps with penciled circles
around blue shapes of water
lie on the dash like Bibles
next to a plastic Jesus,
their car a shimmering cubicle of faith.
Children smile from the backseat
like a church choir.
They hold their hands out the windows
to wave goodbye,
skin stretched tightly over bones
like tiny sails filled with blood and light.

In late afternoon the roads out of here
shine like gold—shimmering veins of hope
that might take us anywhere:
to rain falling thick on corn

green and eight feet tall,
to gray sky fractured wetly on the window.

Tonight in the heat that smothers us
we'll lie awake in our bed,
try to keep our bodies from touching,
and listen as the fingernail moon
falls on our farm to rattle and scratch
through the bones of our fields.

Faith

Our trees have dropped their leaves like litter
on the rusty lawn, but it's only late July.
Outside town this morning
farmers gathered in a field to pray for rain.
Our flowers sold their colors to the wind
a month ago, when locals laid off from their jobs
headed north to New York or Michigan.

The streetlight makes our front porch hold a glow
we drowse in, fanning mosquitoes from our bodies.
We survive with ice in our drinks,
glasses mopped across our faces.
A baseball game scratches out from our old radio
but it's the raspy gray electric rain
in episodes of static from distant heat lightning
that we listen to like prophecy.

Moths swirl like snow,
captive to the light above the street.
Something holds us here in these shadows.
Even in the glow
we can hardly find each other's eyes.

Evidence

My wife and I hold hands
in the little Presbyterian church above the swale
between the highway and the apple hill
among twenty-five others—dresses and overalls,
sweatshirts and parkas, work boots and low heels—
for the candlelight service on Christmas Eve.

At the pastor's urging, people speak their thanks
for whatever God has given them.
One lady near the front says she is thankful
God has brought visitors to their church—
meaning me and my wife.
So I speak up and say on behalf of the visitors
that we're happy to be there and to be part of that company.

In a candlelit silence
I start thinking about the Christmas card
inscribed by a well-meaning friend:
"If you were arrested for being a Christian,
would there be enough evidence to convict you?"

The candle flame in my wife's small hand
trembles and wavers, as if not sure.
I hold my own there beneath hers
until it grows strong again,
the way I would give her anything.

As we leave, a lady hands us a brown paper bag
with an apple, orange, and tangerine,
loose nuts and candy in the bottom:
gifts of the Magi we'll feed the kids for breakfast.

We button our coats and walk out
below the blue neon cross above the door
into the crystal night of stars,
the candle breath and light of baby Jesus
still in our stricken faces.

We drive home holy, holding hands,
singing Christmas with each other,
born again, this between us,
the only evidence we need.

Moving Under Indirect Fire

His small face pressed flat against the door screen,
my son calls me to his play
to see dead soldiers scattered on our lawn,
to see him clasp his chest,
then his practiced pirouette
from porch to walk to shrub,
how his plastic rifle falls just out of reach.
Somehow I think I am supposed to praise him
for this.

Some nights our porch becomes a prow
the darkness laps against in a strange place
where trees are draped with wire and body parts.
The floorboards creak beneath my step.
I turn and do not recognize
the face reflected in the window.

My hand curls again to hide
the burning end of a cigarette.
My throat constricts to whisper.
I hear shrill voices calling
from a shoreline I can almost see.

Some nights I dream I'm back home
sleeping beside my brother.
The soft droning of the window fan
becomes my mother's voice
filling the next room with hymns.

Rain

Four years of drought.
Now we have rain.
Rain too late for last season's crop
keeps this one in the fields.

The new John Deere, not paid for,
sits stiffly rusting in the shed.
Used to be our fathers might lose
one cow each season.
Now it's a farm in every county.

We have forgotten what to say,
so we mumble over cups of coffee
around our kitchen tables
about the ones who haven't quit,
about the reasons not to,
or to go ahead, sell out
before we lose it all.

Outside the church on Sunday,
old men in older ritual
light each other's cigarettes and pipes
and fill the stained-glass air
with words of crops and cattle.
Smoke lifts from their faces,
forever turned to sky and clouds.

We fill our mouths with words
as we try to find a language
for understanding God,

for believing in the miracles
held out above our heads.

The last of my wife's egg money
shimmers above the offering plate,
a small weak candle
burning in her fist.

Third Missed Payment

I feed the horses, make sure of dry hay.
In the house my wife moves against the light.
In the den, scattered across the braided rug,
our kids are at their homework
while the TV gives the evening news to no one.

The old windmill erected by my grandfather
whirls its blades against the red edge of the world.
In the dusk of winter we are surrounded.
At the edge of the woods, darkness unfolds early
to take the fields.

Chapter 2

In What Light

Good Rabbit Dogs

Shotgun cradled in the crook of his arm,
my father waved from the snow-covered rise.
His canvas hunting jacket bulged with unlucky rabbits.
He turned to whistle the beagles from the field.

With a sharp pocketknife I met him outside the shed.
He handed me the jacket.
While he penned the hounds, I reached in,
withdrew the limp warm cloths of fur.

The bowl of salty water turned red.
For a few minutes, smoking his pipe,
he stood beside me. "Here, like this," he'd say—
grim, but somehow joyful.

We weren't poor people, but he was raised that way
and this was only right.
When I asked about it, he looked across the field,
wiped his hands on his pants and said,
"Every morning the world is created new,"
and he strode into the house to my mother.

Good summers of rain, high grasses,
meant fat rabbits at the edge of winter.
The hounds wailed happiness
every time my father neared their pen.

Powerhouse

Descending into the smoky basement
of the powerhouse, at the railing
above the rows of heavy pumps,
above the roar of horses galloping beneath the earth,
I've come here to find my father, the millwright,
among sweating iron men
who toil in half-lit incandescence,
each one's manifest destiny glistening on his brow—
men who accept relentlessly
their portioned unrelenting sameness,
their banishment from the Garden taken, final,
men who have not turned back
from God's cold passion for revenge.

I stand here above them,
dark shadows curling from their faces.
I stand amazed, see how they drag their bodies
into each slight detail of machinery and labor,
how tomorrow is today and yesterday.

Iron men rusting toward the end,
my father stands tall among them,
somehow a music in his body,
the way he stood on our porch at night
as moon and stars walked up the stream
beyond the wood fence.
To hear him say,
"Great men die in turn, one by one.
The merely good fall in mass."
When I tell him I don't understand,
he doesn't try to make me.

Homecoming

Along the rows of knee-high corn
the sunlight entered him
as if through an open window,
the world around him brightening
with what he loved intensely:
turned soil, water, sky,
and everything that lives.

Celebration he walked into each day,
a homecoming he walked into, content,
beloved with his beloved,
fulfilled within the rippled sea of green.
The breathing earth bowed,
bending to the pleasure of his vision.

While all around him men grew old
in their complaining, he walked ageless
through those green rows where I—
no more than the boy I was—
stood apprehended in his light.

White Boat

This must be some mistake,
my strong father lying here,
arms and legs not working,
the small accidents of his life gathered up
in one explosion in his brain.
His voice, like a boy's kite tangled in its lines,
flips on itself upside down.

Mother, beside him, moves gently
in her weariness amid the wires and tubes
rigged across white sheets like folded sails.
Her small kingdom of Heaven has been shaken,
the rivers are running backward,
the sun is stormed with darkness.

Eyes closed, Bible open on her lap
like a helmsman's chart, waypoints lost,
she is redefining course
by stars and the word of light.
Her faith, a small white boat,
holds my father just off shore.

Aftershave

Having shaved my father, adrift
in the cold rage of the nursing home,
I lay my face against his
to test the smoothness of his cheek.
For a moment I hold us together
the way he would when he'd come into my room
to say goodnight.
And the way I would have followed him,
he follows me with his eyes as I turn away.

I walk quickly down the hall
past the reaching arms of others,
frost of their uncharmed faith
stretching from their hands.
I walk past them all, aloof and inexhaustible,
my father's aftershave clinging to my face.
I walk past them all, cool as ice
that breaks loose from its own shore
and, breaking, falls away.

Millwright

Don't look at his right hand, still,
wrapped and pinned in a dishtowel for warmth,
needing five times each hour someone
to adjust the covers, prop a pillow at his back.
That hand held wrench and rule,
made metal think precision, torque, and tolerance.

Don't think of his leg sawn off above the knee
or the breathless mewing of asbestos
in his rattled dreams.

Think of the man who worked overtime
night after sweating night
to put his son through agriculture school,
how he stood there in the half-light of a boiler room
against the strongheart company
and the sweetheart union.

Keep him the man who laughed
behind his welder's mask, the man I saw
in arc-light silhouette through the door of his shop
laying down his calipers and blueprint,
wiping dark grease from his hands
to go out and throw a baseball with his son
against the darkening sky.

Small Thanksgiving

Mother, numb in her exhaustion of caring for my father
settled deep into the clouds of his fourth stroke,
who seven times each night will call her to his bed,
afraid of his incontinence, wishing for the sake of sleep
that he'd accept and just wet the bed,
leans against her shopping cart in the aisles of Hudson's Market.
She selects bread, salt, oatmeal, eggs,
the things she needs for another small Thanksgiving,
another week, until someone comes to sit with him
the hour it takes for her to catch her breath,
to get away long enough to restock her kitchen shelves.

Now she is trying to decide if she wants store-bought cauliflower—
not that it would ever taste of flowered spring in Tennessee
like what my father brought in to our table from his garden,
his rough sunburned hands and face glowing red as a sea captain's
and his smooth whiskey voice bragging we would never find
a garden in the state to match the yellow blooms already set
on his tomatoes, or the corn that would lay so sweet in late July
it would make us weep for more,
when neighbors would bring their lawn chairs to sit beneath
the cicada-singing maples in our yard, where our fathers raced
at shucking ears, the women scraped with butcher knives
as wash pans filled with corn,
while us kids ran, screamed, cobbed dogs, each other,
until mother's patience thinned, threatening us with death,
and my father's face would shine.
Later, the sun of September squinting his eyes, he would grin
while combined feed corn sifted through his lifted hands
like small gold coins fallen from a prayer.

Mother at the check-out stand nods and tells the Hudsons
how good insurance is such a blessing, how Daddy's sweeter
than in years, how he's getting fat on ice cream,
how his eyes will brighten when she mentions Jesus
and he'll sometimes cry as she reads her Bible to him.

I bend to wipe applesauce from my father's chin and ask,
Why is it God forgets his flock sometimes?
Where is it in our broken lives
we were ever truly fashioned in the image of a god?
My father, who never was religious, will ask no bargain now
and takes his stand upon his battered fortress wall.
He speaks to me as if to answer, but I cannot understand
his wobbling unknown tongue—like one of our calves
that pushed between strands of new barbed wire,
couldn't free itself and bawled into the night
until I went out and cut the fence away, to wake next morning
understanding only the blood glazed on my hands.
My father casts his head side to side
like our dog one August night drooled trembling
in the light on our back porch and slow-danced his blind head
back and forth, his face full of poison from a copperhead,
and powerless I stand here now as I did then.

Through the dusk my mother's car bears homeward
up the dusty gravel road to the rest of her life and my father's.
She turns in at the fencerow, headlights beaming
small and pitiful, as if there were no place else to go.
As she comes closer, all around me black birds stir
then settle back into my father's empty fields.

Worms

When the strokes finally killed his arms and legs,
stripped him of his angry words
and gave an odd peace to his stare,
we brought my father home to bed.

I put away his garden tools, packed up his guitar
and moved the TV to his room.
A plastic feeder hangs at the window
where he watches birds move back and forth
between the maples and the sill.
He lies just inside, quiet darkness
a thin comforter pulled up over him.

Afternoons when the wind coos
like a mourning dove at his open window,
he watches skirmishes for food
between species he can no longer name.
Dense years of sullen nights fade.
Days of quiet add and multiply.
Mother smiles and tells him what bird sings
on the windowsill.

Tonight beyond the tool shed
I leaned against the furrowed dark
and watched whatever it is
that lumbers across the garden,
bends over the tomatoes
and rustles through the corn,
that does not stand to wipe sweat
from a sunburned face
and does not curse the goddamned worms.

In What Light

In what light, if any, does a man discover
he's been fashioned in the image of a god?

Though He did the trick in the dawn of Genesis,
those fiery Sunday sermons tried hard enough
to convince you otherwise, so it was not there.

And though it came close enough
as your whole life slipped a little sideways,
it was not that warm sunlit afternoon
you slipped your tongue
into the hungry upturned pleasure of another mouth
as eager hands moved beneath your shirt
toward a risk of finding answers.

And it was not that moonlit night
you turned away from the easy answer
and limped back silently
to the sad weight of your ordinary life.

It could not have been
when you signed your father's stake away
in something called a Living Will
as he lay suspended and quiet
in the blinking lights of small machines
in the fragile edges of his life.

And it was not apparent that bright morning
you grabbed the 12-gauge without thought
to defend the children against the rabid dog
that staggered in a growling palsy
from the fields of the next farm,

then carried that limp thing back to your neighbor,
begging his forgiveness.

But it may have been there in the shadows,
in the aftermath of things like those,
the things that call you from the plains
of your ordinary life
into a country inhabited by strangers,
where in one brief circumstance
your capacity for change has been unexpectedly revealed
in some extraordinary doing of something simple.

Or perhaps you might find it
in the awful strength it takes
to go back to the things you have to do,
to the obligations and commitments you made
back in the darkness of your youth,
to the blood oaths you took in the beginning
around small fires in the night,
where you must have believed,
with all your heart believing,
the small light you found there
was all the light you would ever see.

Air Burial

When death leaned over and hissed into my grandfather's face
until the light bled from his eyes
and his bones burned thin within him,
he sat up and said, "Don't bury me as if you could save me."

"Save your money. Drag me out through the woods,
find me a ledge over some gorge with a breeze,
then prop me up to greet the buzzards,
possums, maybe a bear.
Let my bones bleach in the sun a year,
then gather and grind them into meal,
knead the meal into dough, bake two loaves
and take them back as crumbs to scatter on the wind."

Tonight I narrowly missed a raccoon
shuffling across my headlight beams
and I recalled that summer thirty years ago,
going back day after day on my bike
to frighten crows away from the carcass
of a groundhog by the road and to watch
as corn seeds from its belly finally sprouted
out of bleached white bones and hair:

Sprouts greener than anything I'd ever seen
in an endless summer of dark suns and dreams
where vultures circled high and black in a suffocating sky
like ministers of the unburied dead,
grandfather flying with them, a phoenix, eyes sharp and clear,
all his fine new bones green and strong.

Third Generation Farming

The young red bull in our lower pasture
bellows across the sun-swept evening field,
frustration stamped into the dust.
He walks the fencerow constantly,
head turned north, straining the breeze
to rediscover cows across the rise.

He moves heavily, tests the fence posts
with his stubborn head. I envy him,
so sure of what he wants and needs.
For him, this is the law. If he knew
I have the power to open gates,
to free his lust upon any willing cows,
he'd bow his head when I walk by
and he'd look at me with different eyes.

I pull the tractor into the dark shed,
not tired of farming but tired
of the relentless never having enough,
and walk the tenuous beam of light
cast from the kitchen window
back to where the ends always seem to meet.

Early, through the soft breathing
of our still dark house,
I walk out to lean against the gate
where breath ghosts mill about black shapes
of cattle lowing their communal and unspeakable loss.

I go back in, find my small son in the dark
and hold his sleeping body hard against my chest
until I can almost put my hands on what it is.

Chapter 3

Aching Hands

Early Frost

Last month you reminded me
all our friends divorced years ago.
Last night you came home late.
We both pretended sleep.

Today you have followed October's sun
from room to quiet room, not speaking,
wading barefoot and alone
in each small pool of light.

All day you have escaped me,
returning to the windows
for something in the distance.

Beside you at the window,
my hand in the small of your back,
I see below us marigolds
tinged black by early frost,
maple leaves littering the walk.

The woman from the next farm
down the road comes by to say
the coming winter will be hard.
Your hand rises to your lips,
as if to keep yourself from saying
what you have not.

Aching Hands

My best gloves won't stay on for anything,
won't keep these farmer's hands
from growing rough and cracked in the cold
or keep them from aching
in the heat of the woodstove.

I bend an hour over the bathroom sink,
scouring black dirt and grease
from knuckles and fingernails,
rubbing hand cream into my palms
and thinking of your breasts warm and sleek
beneath the red satin gown from Christmas.

At last I stand here naked in the dark
beside our bed, hands rubbed raw and clean,
listening to the lightness of your breath
as your comfortable breasts rise and fall
in sleep.

Last night I dreamed about your new boss—
the way he smiles at you, the way you talk of him,
how his hands are smooth and warm
as the light in polished cedar.

Toast

Driving fast on I-65 North from Nashville
beneath the same sun that shines golden
on the shores of Italy and France and Spain,
as the yellowed dust floats out toward a gentle autumn,
from the on-ramp behind me comes to pass
a purple Ford pickup truck.

How can I come to instant hatred
just because this man drives a truck
like the one driven by a man who has set himself
as my enemy?
And thinking of it, knuckles white and ready
on the wheel, I almost do it to him
into the bridge abutment there—
Wham! Teeth and bone in concrete,
the smell of blood smeared with creosote,
hair merged with windshield glass,
the radio blaring a still pissed-off Merle Haggard,
my own life suddenly condensed and well.

Then, knowing I could do it, I don't.
Stiff and smug, I let him pass, safe,
and see it's someone else entirely,
some sweet old farmer from Kentucky
with an old brown dog smiling on the seat beside him,
head poked out the window.
I relax and breathe it out.

When I get home, it's still on my mind
and my hatred curls like a mangy dog
in the sun in August, biting

at the impossible boils on his ass.

Cursing, I raise a cold one from the fridge

to the guy I didn't kill today,

then another to all the ones I have.

Half-Light Off the Appalachian Trail

After hours of waiting for the rain to lift,
I walk behind you down Ledbetter Ridge
from Russell Field to Cades Cove,
our last day on the crest.
Used to be these trips would heal our wounds,
make us close again, but this whole week
has been sodden with damp conversation,
the sky laden with clouds obscuring every view.

I follow on, watching the sky darken for another storm,
wondering if we've saved anything.
Oncoming hikers, a couple headed for the top,
stop to ask how far.
Forty-five minutes for us to walk down
means two more hours for them to reach the top.
Friendly talk—the first in days—of destinations,
packs, good shoes, the proper gear for rain.
Finally glancing at watches,
saying they want to make shelter before dark,
then groaning and sighing they bend forward
in the self-imposed traces of backpackers
and move away, trudging upward in the half-light.

I drive home as if alone, blind in rain
and headlights, you far away in stillness
on your dark side of the truck,
the wipers slapping rhythm to the cold silences
piling up between us like a mountain
we can't see over, can't climb, won't try
as long as it's raining.

Moon with Crow

Across our farm in each of six dark ponds
swims a silver moon.
Up drinking before dawn,
I count them—six of them—
each one slightly farther from the shore.

Red spars of morning light
lean across the tops of trees,
the green depths and fields awake
to their everyday swirling dance.
A woman can be like that.

The ponds of night burst into flame
like magicians' plates of fire
where folded messages from the audience
disappear, then reappear
as white doves in the hand
that blaze up for a moment
like a love affair.

I knew a woman once
with yellow hair
like moonlight spilling.
I would have followed her
anywhere.

A single black crow races against itself
into the trees where the night must go
to cower.

A man can be like that,
nursing the dark wound in himself

in silence—

until he is right,

until there is nothing else to say.

Tim's Watercolor

The clear water appears to be green
because it's reflecting perfectly
the entire green heart of the trees
in the mushroomed leaf-yard on the other side.

Sometimes I wade in,
away from wood smoke and melancholy.
Dog-paddle out,
swim the thirty-nine strokes across, then
climb out onto the angled roundish surface
of white stone clasped by the tree line
so gently you might not notice.

There I feel the sudden bird-snap
of rhododendron breeze against wet skin.
In the hard fact of the stone, I sit still
in that patch of sun and watch
the cluster of white dogwood blooms
unfold their egret wings
from the dark loop of the cove
to scribble their names above swarming minnows.

A few steps beyond the beech tree
that leans away from the others
as if against an old storm,
beyond a mat of pine needles
there is a mossy thickness
where I follow the dimpled prints of hooves
to a trail and find tracks of a large bear.
I never get to the shadowed edge of danger
before I turn around.

Still I imagine there is a small village in the sun
just behind that last dark span of woods
where there is music and laughter,
where my name is remembered,
where I would be welcomed after years of absence.

Susan

I am thinking about a girl from 20 years ago
named Susan
who had a boyfriend in the Air Force.
I wish I had met her for our solitary picnic
behind the girls' gym on graduation night
like I promised.

And I wonder if she went back there,
happy in the dark,
and I wonder how long she may have stood there,
nervous in her graduation gown and cap,
looking at her tin Timex watch
as the close railroad cars rumbled south
on the L&N line to Nashville,
ice melting in the cups of Pepsi, fingernails
manicured for the biggest night of her life
clutching that paper bag filled with hamburgers
and french fries from Perk's Drive-In.

Susan of wink and grin
and reach across the aisle and pinch,
who admired my bad handwriting,
who laughed at my stupid jokes,
who shared the chocolate chip cookies from Home Ec,
small blonde goddess of Miss Phipps' geography class
who loved the magic names of faraway places with me,
I'm sorry I stood you up.
Call me if you read this.

I have been to war.
I've been shot down in flames.

I've been drunk.

Susan, I've been to the places we talked about.

I have things to tell you.

Making Pearls

Because you wore his ring on a chain around your neck
and someone else wore mine,
our trips to this beach were always just as friends.
But suntan oil is an elixir of touch,
an aphrodisiac too strong for high school loyalties.
One warm night we stayed after dark
and left the top of your two-piece drifting in the surf.
You laughed about how grains of biting sand
folded within soft flesh make pearls.
We drove sixty miles past the exit to our town
before you said,
"No, we have commitments we must honor."

Today, half a lifetime and a family later,
I drive back here and catch myself
looking for the top of that leopard skin two-piece,
wanting to write you messages in the sand,
half-expecting you to show—
as if years of going back to our commitments
could be erased in a single swirling of the tide
and we might drive on into the night,
not ever looking back,
as if fingers slick with oil
could ever grasp and keep that perfect one
from a basket full of pearls.

Destinations

Searching through these travel brochures for some place I can't find,

my mind hangs on an ad with a photo of a red tractor

that pulls you to me in the backseat

of my father's old red-and-white Fairlane Ford

parked back on Fox's farm on a Sunday afternoon

in a field of sunflowers—

the polished chrome gleaming,

the yellow air speckled with radio static, clicking locusts,

floating motes of dust and pollen, backlit insect wings,

white moths hung in long slow shafts of light

filtered down through dark leaves and limbs

of the live oak tree we called ours that summer

dappling us with gold—

the fine hairs gold on your shoulders

and gold in the small of your back against the deepness of your tan,

your dove-soft breasts thrust high, your blonde hair thrown back

across the seat, eyes squinted shut,

the woven plastic seat cover imprinting a faint red filigree

on the goldleaf of your thighs,

small beads of sweat gilding your swollen lips with light,

your quick hands guiding my sex to your sex,

to that sudden tremble, your liquid summer voice shuddering

"There it is...."

Chapter 4

God, If You Are There

Circus

Father, the knife thrower, doubled as a whiskey-drinking clown
with a big red nose. Mother, our fire-eating sword swallower,
juggled several things at once and danced.
And hovering just above the ceiling was God,
the black-caped ringmaster with a top hat and a whip.

Shadow characters were my best act.
Elephants, lions, tigers performed nightly on the noisy wall
beside the bed that held me and my big brother.
We walked the high-wire tightrope heel to toe
for the three of them, no net below.

Whitewashing the Blues

I wanted to be like Elvis.
My mother wanted me to be Pat Boone.
She bought me smooth white buckskin shoes
and a white sport coat
that I wore to Sunday school,
hands jammed deep into my trouser pockets.

Those buckskin shoes looked like
big dumb-ass white balloons
floating out in front of me with each step I took.
They would get scuffed and dirty
and when I tried to wipe the dirt off
against my navy blue pants leg,
the white would come off onto the navy blue—
the phoniness of that whitewash obvious
to everyone, it seemed to me, but my mother.

She pushed my hair up from my eyes
while she lectured me about clean living,
about the image I presented to a world
already rocking with guys like Elvis and Little Richard,
a world already teetering toward anarchy,
as if she did not know
all the Pat Boones in the world
in their clean white buckskin shoes
and white sport coats—
all the whitewash in the world—
was not enough to save us.

Kept Photos

In this one from the family album,
he stands at the top of the playground slide,
small knuckles white around the rails.
His hair lifts from his forehead in Tennessee sunlight.
His eyes said then what you already knew:
Such a sharp drop so fast!

So you smiled and reassured him:
 "You'll be all right....Go ahead....
Let go....Don't be afraid."

In this one, years later, a night photo from the war,
he stands leaning slightly forward in the tall grass
at the lip of death's inkwell
filled with sounds of dying in the jungle.
The boy who sent the photo stands a few steps off,
strained face to the camera, mouth open,
appears to shout—but from too far, too far—

everything he knows, everything he might say:
"Go ahead, be afraid,"
his voice too small against the roar.

Escape

In my childhood I was surrounded by people wanting to escape.
My father was escaping his lack of education
and the Great Depression
and carried the fear like a chip on his shoulder
like he carried the machinist's rule he could barely read
in his oil-stained khakis
and voted Democrat every chance he got.

My mother was escaping her childhood
as a real-life Cinderella
with a wicked stepmother
who would beat her with a spatula
that left red welts across her cheek.

My grandparents were the same, escaping
their farm's foreclosure by selling out early,
abandoning the family graveyard
and taking jobs for minimum wage in the city.

My Sunday school teacher was escaping
the bees in her bonnet, an abusing husband,
the wringing of her chapped hands
and something she called the sin in her life.

I was their pathway out.
My mother still calls me in the middle of the night
to say she is depending on me.
And I have tried to be that path for all of them
but the madness follows me everywhere I go
and I don't know the way
and there is no madness, or all of it is.

Hanging On

Insanity drops in, uninvited,
smartly gowned in knowledge or religion
or negligéed as love.
It redefines the soul, evicts the tenant,
hears voices in the hall,
falls in lust with lust, speaks in unknown tongues,
double-bolts the door.

Maybe it tears the curtains down,
changes color and style of hair,
forgets to pay the light bill,
takes up herbal tea.

Sometimes it weeps at night when the family is asleep,
plots the perfect crime, stares wistfully for hours
at patterns veined in leaves,
at the etching of years reflected in the mirror.

The children aren't exactly children.
They're obligations, paid against forever
like perpetual layaway.
Takes all you have remaining

while insanity searches the mail in desperation
for the name of Current Occupant.
You know nothing will separate you
from your suicide.

The animals hiding in the closet
and underneath the bed
watch the slots of light go dark,
breathe long slow sighs of relief
and hold their ears against the floor.

Home Baking

(for mother)

"Sister and I laughed too much.
Stepmother slapped me with the tin spatula
we gave her for Christmas.
I fought the tears, went out to the barn,
climbed up cold thick rungs,
pressed my face down hard
against the gray boards of the dark loft,
felt spatula slots burn and swell and ooze
like red slugs across my cheek.

I peered through the cracks,
squinted against the brightness of the snow
and watched sister look for me in the hedge,
listened to her call from the back porch all afternoon
until the snow began to glisten pink,
until father came home tired and dark.
I would not cry, especially then.

And I knew in the warm house
sister would be snug at father's knee,
his big hard hand stroking her brown hair,
stepmother behind him in the ritual kneading
of his thick neck, a smile across his face,
the smell of baking heavy in the air."

Orchard Voices

A farmer's daughter, she had seen it all:
the flowers' careless colorings and scents
cast to and fro, the bees' insane roaring
in the apple trees,
the insolent nuzzling of the stallion
among the willing mares,
the arrogant shoving of the bull upon the cows—
purposeful matings the natural order—
the casualness of it all.

Her summer afternoons in the cool air of the river
beneath the trees with the farmhand's son
seemed just as natural. Then the marriage at 17,
the piece of land, the plowing, planting,
rain and sun, the first pregnancy
ending in the fall down cellar stairs
and dismal burial in the orchard
of an unnamed dark-eyed girl,
the black despair that everyone said would heal eventually
and so it seemed as other children came.
There was so much life around her
the shady orchard became a place for walks alone.

Two sons have gone away.
Her husband died three years ago.
She walks in fallen apple blossoms
like snow under the unkept trees
and thinks how one life is lived half-trapped in another
and she imagines a naked unnamed child glistening

in the roots, sliding through the trees, wanting out,
trying to call out through the leaves...Mother....

Sometimes she sits here with all the flowers fallen
while so green at heart
and bends to touch her face against the soft spring grass
just to feel it breathe.

Children's Graves in the Back of Our Farm

Four crude rows of slanting stones
nestle in leaves under oak and beech—
stones rusted green with lichen heraldry,
names of children stuttered faintly
above chiseled claims that what is gone
is not forgotten.

How could we have missed so long
so much loss plainly lying here?
Where we have blindly searched for cow and calf,
where we have spent, with wine and bread and games,
high laughing summer afternoons,
the earth was opened to accept the loss of others
and we never saw it till now.

I pondered through the fall
how twelve small graves could lie untended—
how in all that green place
honeysuckle runs amuck with blue-eyed grass
and periwinkle flits like butterflies among the stones,
how death has been abandoned to the woods
and is no more permanent than life.

In this winter light, as I watch my children
move within the warm shadows of our home,
as branches crack in icy skins,
as root and bone shift earth toward spring,
in tops of trees at our farm's edge
stark thin fingers point to God.

God, If You Are There

The Little League mother screams at her son again,
the tall and lanky shortstop
who has just made his third error of the game:
"Stay in front of it!...Keep your head in, idiot!...
Don't drop your back shoulder, boy—you're stepping out!"

Her jowls sag and flutter
at the top of her heavy stinking body
she covers with a sack dress with flowers printed on it.
Everybody knows if her boy can make the all-star team,
she will be an all-star too.

The Little League fathers stand shoulder to shoulder
at the urinals, never looking to the side
but only at the wall straight ahead
where her name appears in graffiti jest:
FOR A GOOD TIME CALL

I caught a four-pound bass and cleaned it in my kitchen sink
and took the bloody head and tail and bones and slimy innards
to her mailbox and dropped it in.
Of course she blamed her son and beat him in the yard
while the neighbors stood there watching from their porches.

A new town is being built
in the blue-green hills of southern Kentucky.
They are going to call it Heaven.
I have already applied for the position of town drunk.
If it's not too late to save Himself, God should save us too.

House on Berry Street

On the way to visit relatives in their new house
where they expect to live happily ever after,
I drive a block off Hadley on 13th to Berry
to show the kids where I was born.

Cars at the curb narrow the street to one lane
and boys on bikes dart out from the old walk
as if every driver in the world should know
this street belongs to kids.
A mother leans out her window, yells time for supper.
An invisible child playing somewhere up the street
yells back.

The old townhouse is lit
and we can see the shadows of a family
moving through the light like wings.
A baby cries and a woman drifts cloud-like
from the dining room to the hall that leads back
to the room where I was locked at night.

In tears, I watch the bar of light below the door
ease into the room like a silent secret friend.
I lie there breathing the cool air next to the floor
until mother leaves the house.
The slot of light goes dark and cold,
swelling into something large like God.

I don't tell my kids in the backseat about that.
Instead I laugh and tell them
how I could lean against the wall in my closet
and hear the funny boy next door holler every night
while his mother washed his ears.

The Others

Sometimes I can almost feel them,
rustling in the dark
like animals on softly padded feet
moving through high grass:
the others I could have been,
the sleek happiness of them.

Sometimes I sense them waiting,
sprawled and napping on the shaded limbs of trees,
like children who have learned patience
waiting for their supper
or soldiers standing on a platform
listening for the train.

Sometimes I see them glazed in grime,
half-naked, wild and trembling in their heat,
lurking in the woods across the road.

Often, like tonight at the old house,
clouds peeling off the moon,
I can make out some of them,
like the one innocent in his schoolboy clothes,
no stitch-scar signature below the eye

or the one glistening with sex, confident as stone,
incredulous, staring back at me
from the patch of light at the corner of the street,
who has circled close
but never raised his hand in greeting:
the one who would not be me,
the one I dream I am.

In the Attic

In the attic of my father's house
I find things I had forgotten:
pieces of a childhood layered with dust,
filed in a cardboard box
for private viewing with a microscope.

I find no photos made of me
like there were of my older brother
except the yearly ones from school
and one of those my mother tore
and threw away

because it magnified her belief
that I was terminally asthmatic:
sitting on the front row, my arms
thrust down out of too-large sleeves—
impossible stilts to hold lungs
up in the air.

It was painful for her to see it
framed inside clean white borders
among the healthy classmates
I knew so little of—
less of than my doctors, but more of
than the sister who died before me,

the one whose death paved a way for me
with the dark fear of loss.
What may go is best not recorded,
not bound to walls with wire
as shrines for pain or pasted in albums
to serve up on rainy days.

Still, here in this dark attic
some joy is stored:
plastic Roy Rogers
with missing hand and six-gun...
Trigger's tail is gone
with the bridle and saddle
somewhere long ago.

The construction set that entertained
more hours of training than a university
lies quiet and dusty
beneath plastic-bagged stacks
of Superman comics that brag
Still Only 10 Cents!

An almost new bat,
a too well-oiled mitt
reliving some few easy days of hot sun
and bare chest that sounded normal:
a beat-out bunt
and one well-turned double play,
talked about for years.

The scrapbook on South America
that earned an A+ in fifth grade,
the gas-engined Piper Cub
still suffering from an early death
met on the baseball field
just after one bright Christmas

and the old red aluminum pitcher
that used to sweat icy cold

on still August nights and make a river
that would crawl across the dark and touch
the vast plain of dreaded silence
in my father's fingers

that gripped the table's edge
as he wished he could not hear,
above the clear-aired chirp of frog
and cricket outside the screened window,
the rasp and rattle emerging
from the bedroom down the hall.

Chapter 5

Enough

Farmer's Market

I'm driving to town, bushels of sweet corn
in my old pickup
rusting into its own planned obsolescence
while the maladjusted lifters clatter
in the head and the worn-out clutch
grinds and grabs and whines
each time I force another gear.

Construction narrows the freeway to one lane
where the traffic thickens and binds
like our stupid cows in the barn at milking time.
So I take the exit at First Street,
stopping at the light beneath the trees
that shade the whores and winos there
in front of the old motels and bars.

I watch these honest whores—who know
everybody pays a price to love or be loved—
standing at the curb in their impartial bodies
wrapped in leather and fishnet stockings,
smoking, brushing hair, leaning in the shadows.

I catch a whiff of dark perfume
and imagine trying to talk to one of them,
how she might call me Doll or Baby
and she'd say, "You're a good-looking guy.
A guy like you shouldn't look so lonely.
Don't you need a little company?"

I'd be embarrassed and I'd say, "No.
Heck, no! I'm married. Don't I look married?"
I'd ask directions for the bridge to downtown,

I'd feel dumber than I look
and those whores would chew and pop their gum
and turn their heads to watch my old truck
tremble into gear and see the flakes of rust
pop off the tailgate as I grind it into second.

But one of them might wonder for a minute
how it would be to live with a farmer
on a place with cows and cats and white chickens,
with children and a shade tree in the yard.
Maybe we'd have a neon sign blink
slow and blue across our bed:
NO VACANCY...NO VACANCY

After the market, I drive back by.
The tender whores are gone.
All that's left is one old wino, fine and happy
with his nightly pint and a patch of warm summer grass
beneath his lonely neon landmark
I've grown accustomed to:
NO VACANCY...NO VACANCY

Sanibel Island

These fanatic storms drive sun and bathers
from the beach.
Gulls now stark white knives
skirl through dark sky,
seek shelter in the mangroves of the bay,
where the rain has flushed chameleons
from the limbs and trunks of trees.

Soon what strikes the eye will be
red hibiscus petals scattered on the sand,
chameleons skittering back across the walk,
dunes shifted slightly southward
and new lovers—
who almost notice nothing,
who raise umbrellas on the beach
to hide their burning bodies,
who in their perfect lives
have not yet reckoned storms,
who wear dark lenses and agree:
the heavy clouds massing on the skyline
look like sails of mystic ships.

Reconciliation

After we fight all week, a breeze
stirs calligraphy over the bay.
From the end of our pier, a blue heron
lifts stiffly into the air,
tilts slowly to sea, its great wings heaving
to the sun-red edge of the world.

Rising, you cross the deck to watch,
framing her flight with your hands lifted
as if holding her high on course.
Now on the pier,
the red sun backlighting your hair,
you stand on tiptoe for a moment
and dive into the sky,
the rippled air holding you,
in one of those moments
you had been waiting for, as if all your life.

Christmas Gossip

This too shall pass, I tell myself,
arms full of dried cornstalks, stems of tomato plants,
straw and weeds from the kitchen garden.
I stack them in the middle until there is a huge pile,
big enough for burning.

The women in my life—my wife and her mother—
sit in my house talking the annual Christmas gossip
about every low-class member of the family.
In two days my mother-in-law will leave
with her arms full of Christmas gifts
to stay with another daughter across town,
where she will sit with my sister-in-law
and talk about us, about me:

About how much weight I've gained,
how my garage is a mess a pig could not live in
and a rat would not,
how my automobile is filthy,
how I go about unshaved for days
and wear the same old jeans four days in a row,
how I drink too much,
how I don't discipline my children,
how I don't fold my underwear and handkerchiefs
before I put them away,
how I should try my hand at country music,
how I should get back in church and tithe,
how she doesn't understand how my wife can live with me—

It must be for the kids, they'll agree, and wear it thin
and turn to another son- or daughter-in-law

until they have uncovered every sin of distant aunts and cousins
who never finished high school or held a decent job,
who sponged off their daddies until they finally died
hands up in the air and not much good for anything themselves,
and they will sadly shake their nappy heads in solemn agreement
at the miserable life I have given my wife and kids.

I pile these weeds and cornstalks high, knowing this will pass,
but now I wish I had a stake I could stab into the ground
out there in the middle where I could bind someone
hand and foot—I wish I had the balls to do that
and to stand there before the condemned
like a prophet with a Bible shouting against the wind
the righteous words of God's judgment on gossips and whores,
and I wish I had a match to set them all aflame
in the cornstalks and stems of tomato plants and weeds.

My garden would be clean,
ready for spring.
I might even clean out the garage.
I might shave.
I'd like to see
what they would have to say
about that.

Enough

Through the summer air dad's axe
sliced a sardonic grin of light
into the darkness of the honeysuckle
and ironwood trees.
I took him water and stood back, safe.
I watched the ripple of muscle in his arms,
the swath of sweat spread across his denim shirt,
the white knuckles of his hands,
and wondered how he did it, quietly without stopping.

Welts from thorn and briar cabled his forearms and wrists.
Blood seeped from scratches on the backs of his hands,
red beads that were slung off with each swing.
Mother had complained finally enough. Now he was showing her.
The black-footed red fox in our fencerow
would not come back for years.

He was like that. He never said a word about anything,
just did what it took to make my mother's voice ease off.
But when he would stop his merry whistle,
the wink, the hand wiping sweat from his grin,
you knew darkness bred in him
and lightning would strike the highest point.
That kind of thing didn't happen often,
but when it did, the rest of us laid low.

That summer, as mother found more and more
to complain about, dad would go out in the evenings
to sit and smoke his pipe beneath our largest maple.
From there he could see the moonlit field
where the fireflies wheeled

with their green flickering elements of truth.

And beyond the field, he watched the highway

where red taillights streaked away

through the darkness on their way to somewhere else.

Blue Light

In these photos from the shoe box
kept deep beneath my mother's bed,
here is my father with his jazz band,
face glowing in a soft blue nightclub light,
his slicked blonde hair combed up
and the sleeves of his crisp white shirt rolled up.

And, God, he is smiling—almost laughing.
And there in his hands are those sticks
he kept time with on the snare
and there is the bass drum that beat like a heart
and bore his nickname, Dink,
scrawled across the front.

My father looks at home in that haven
of smoke and beer and guitar riffs and rhythm
and soft blue light that filters down
through a smoky Heaven or up from Hell
or wherever it is from.

What the photo doesn't show is my mother:
young, sober, grim-faced, maybe scowling
from a table in the back
behind those girls up there dancing close
against the men in that blue light,
skirts twirling a bit too high
for a married woman's comfort,
their sweet perfume twisting away from them
through that lonely saxophone.

The photo doesn't show those velvet women
who lived their lives with buttons open,

straps undone, hooks already loose,
soft good times in nylons and garters:
women who could lead a man out
to the dark backseat of an automobile,
women who knew the easy weaknesses of men,
could trap them like a spider traps a fly.

The photo doesn't say
how even a good man can be tempted
to perform the unholy, the profane,
how a man might never go home
to his good wife and children,
how it might be my father giving up his soul
and my mother who would pay the price.

No, the photo doesn't show my mother
or the good-time girls, the dangerous ones,
or anyone in need of being saved.
It only shows my father, happy,
a few years before the rest of his life.
In this photo—in this one—he is smiling
in his music and his rhythm
in that blue light—smiling
as if his life was something special,
as if his life was something good.

Lilith

She took Adam by the hand and led him to the stream
and the bed of ferns where she wrapped her golden legs
and arms around him.
She showed him how to use his lips,
his tongue, his teeth, his whole ecstatic body
in their simple act of worship.
They took each other with aggression:
as gluttons take a meal with greed,
the way a horse will drink with such pleasure
it will founder.
Then they sprawled among the ferns
like the lions beneath the trees,
who would flick their tails and yawn contentedly.

In the afternoon, Adam rose and stretched out his arms
to embrace his wonderful life.
He named a dozen animals
but soon grew bored and turned to look for her.
The animals without names sighed
and stood in line, waiting patiently at first.
But as the days went by, the ones with names
began looking down their noses at the ones without.
Fights broke out. Whole named and unnamed species
were wiped off the earth.

But God was watching. He was watching
like a cigar-smoking foreman in a factory,
like a time and motion study man.
He watched until he could not stand it anymore,
then made Adam sleep,

wiped his memory cleaner than a Disney film
and woke him up with Eve

who lay there on her back,
arms and legs out straight
as she let Adam do it to her
while she talked and talked and talked
about the crop that needed planting,
the beans that needed hoeing,
about the quiet time and prayer
they should save for Him.

Adam finished quickly,
reached up for a fig leaf
and slouched out to weed the garden,
trying to remember what made him love the ferns,
what made him sigh
as if his heart was full of sorrow.
There was something missing from his life,
he could feel it in his bones.

Requiem in Room 10

Eyes closed to the innocence
cracked and peeling like old icons,
she sighs her breathless prayer:
"Never before have I been...
so exactly where I want to be."

New at this, I lie, "Me too! Me too!,"
roll over on my side, stare past my past
into the bathroom where my shadow turns,
grins in false collusion, stifles a laugh,
jams his finger down his throat,

crosses his eyes, rolls them back in his head
until it hurts. He thumbs down his underwear
and moons me, grabs the lamb-white towel
from its corner of the tub, wads it up
and stuffs it in his mouth.

Winking at me now, he tears the crucifix
from his neck, holds it tenderly
over the fake-marble sink,
pulls a toothbrush out of the air,
begins to scrub and scour

until it bleeds and bleeds, spatters mirror,
window, ceiling light, and floor—
all too much for the thin white wafer
lying there wrapped in clean wax paper,

the thin wafer of absolution
for dissolving between hands
or bitterly on the tongue,

the one always waiting there
on the edge of motel sinks,

replaced in daily ritual
by some unseen hand.
Some I save, like souvenirs,
take home, collect for some day
I might need them.

Fixing Her Mowing Deck

I'm leaning over her lower parts
with my fingers jammed down deep,
slick and oily in the dark, so tight
I'm sure to break at least one
before I come out, that screw lost
in her PTO.

It smells like musky grass down here
where the work is done, and I'm dizzy
in this heat and something is making her
hump up and down and vibrate apart
and my fingers are aching and I'm feeling

this fly crawl over my back, biting
and stinging, I'm getting a cramp
but I can't quit now—something tells me
she's about to turn over
and go like never before.

Scythe

I've laid enough reluctant money
on God's offering plate
to pay for a stout boat
I could have sailed away on.

The blue in my eyes was once the color
of a calm sea over white sand.
Once my smile was genuine
and my belly was flat.
My legs were muscular,
my mother always said.

Daddy's mood swings
cut her heart strings like a scythe,
and lack of love, she said,
did the rest.

My brother could hit a baseball
over the railroad tracks behind center field.
Once the ball landed in a coal car
and went to Canada, I think.

I discovered a girl back there once.
She was crouched in the weeds,
her clothes were torn and she was weeping.
I did not speak of it to anyone
until now.

She could have been my mother,
I don't know.

Recalling the Names of Constellations

Tonight as I sat smoking one last cigarette,
the moon suspended like God's clipped fingernail
above Pettigo's Hill, the names of constellations
took me by surprise—recalled after twenty years
from the night when a girl, who would later have my kids,
unhooked her bra and promised me, as I promised her,
that we'd be lovers forever.
As the stars rose to their slow dance
beyond the firefly swirl above us, we renamed the clusters:
First Base, Second, Mystical Ship, Lovers, God's Fingernail.
Orion became Old Ryan, then Farting Henry.

I scaled the ladder of the water tank above the park
to spray-paint bold and black:
DAN + SALLY JANE 1969 FOREVER
while she sat watching from the car,
her trembling hands my reward.

Now it seems eerie to remember—
after separate lives arose almost unnoticed,
distinct and silent across the widening plain
from Madison to Oxbow, across all the people in between,
after all the risings of Cassiopeia, Cepheus, Perseus—
that night we held on for all we were worth
in the backseat of my father's Ford Galaxie.

The water tower was torn down years ago,
the Galaxie traded for a pickup.
And we have traveled far, or not.
The earth has spun a little larger, a little crazier,

tilted a little farther on its side.
We forgot to remember our constellations.

But somewhere, light years down inside,
we've come back around, stars ourselves.
After all that space and time we are the same once more,
and we recall, in the magic of one split second,
whatever we recall.

Acknowledgments

I owe deep gratitude to Brian Daly, my publisher and editor, who kept this book of poems honest. He's the man who has made it work. And to those good friends and willing hands who reviewed and commented on the manuscript: Bill Brown, Richard Fox, Mickey Hall, Jim Holder, Vol Lindsey, Marilyn Johnson, Klyd Watkins, Amy Daly, Jamie Givens, Chris Daly, and my son, Cody. Thanks to each of you. Thanks also to Laura Clemons at Tennessee Tech University for providing the author photo, and to my brother, Don, for his support.

About the Author

DAN POWERS performed in the acclaimed PBS TV special, *The United States of Poetry*, with Nobel and Pulitzer Prize winners Derek Walcott, Joseph Brodsky, Czeslaw Milosz, and Allen Ginsberg. His poems have been published in *New York Quarterly, Wormwood Review, Cumberland Poetry Review, Pearl*, and other leading publications. He co-edited and appeared in *Something We Can't Name*, an anthology of Nashville's open-mike poetry readings.

Powers hails from Neely's Bend, Tennessee, where, he says, "Men are judged by the size of their tires." An electrical engineer by trade and a farmer by heritage, he retired from the Tennessee Valley Authority in 2002. This is his first full-length collection.